Skydiving Without a Parachute and Other Success Stories

Brooke Gerbers

Copyright © 2024 Poets Underground Press LLC

All rights reserved.

Poets Underground Press LLC

poetsundergroundpress.com

Publication by
Poets Underground Press LLC
on August 1st, 2024

Cover Design & All Illustrations by Kyra Rolleri

No part of this book may be reproduced, stored in a retrieval system or transmitted by any means without the consent of the publisher and/or the contributors.

The views expressed in this book of poems are solely those of the Writer and do not necessarily reflect the views of the Publisher, and the Publisher hereby disclaims any responsibility for them.

ISBN: 979-8-218-47844-5

Table of Contents

Foreword	6
Allow Me to Introduce Myself	7-8
Unapologetically Woman	9
Nightly Routine	10
But Don't Call Me Weak	11
Take Me Out of My Skin	12-13
Pretty in Pink	14-15
How to Write Poetry	16
Whiskey or Lighter Fluid	17
2,000 Days in Recovery	18-19
How to Survive a Gunshot Wound (When You're the One that Pulls the Trigger)	20
To the Trees Outside the Window, I Could See if it wasn't so Dark	21
The First One on Grief	22-23
We All Get Out Alive and Other Lies I Tell Myself	24
Track Star	25-26
I Call it Going Back, She Calls it Coming Home	27-28
Among the Unlikable Parts	29
Photo Album Confessions	30
I Love You but…	31-32
If the Timing were Right, the Story Would be Boring	33
Don't Talk to Me About the Weather	34

Holier than Thou	35
On Tattoos and Apologies	36
Butch Church Girl	37
Playing Dress Up	38-39
Black Sheep	40
The Body Keeps Score	41
Learned Behavior	42-43
Under a Microscope	44
Things to do Between the Hours of 12 and 1 AM	45
Almost Untouchable	46
Fantasizing about the Men in the Room	47-48
Before You Say Yes	49
Evidence that You're Alive	50
The Talk of the Century	51
Shit No One Actually Cares About	52
First Date Confessions	53
Playing Hide and Seek with Yourself	54
Steps to Making a House a Home	55
Steps to Making a House a Home: Part 2	56
Urn	57
Finding a Means to an End	58-59
First Date and a U-Haul	60
When We Ask Why	61-62
Surviving on Scraps	63
Construction Site	64
Mouth or Muzzle	65-66
An Astronaut's Love Letter	67-68

Loving in My Mother's Language	69
Weathering the Storm	70
Life is Silly	71-72
10 Places You Can Find Me	73
If I Should Ever Go Missing	74
A Love Letter to My Hips	75
Happy Poem	76
Between Slab City and Salvation	77-78
Kintsugi	79
First Step	80
Other Firsts	81
Cheers to the End of the Patriarchy	82
Soul City	83-84
I Have to Tell You…	85
Correction: Not a Fever Dream	86-87
A Love Letter to Myself	88-89
I am Poet	90-91
I Never Asked to be a Survivor	92
Supernova	93-95
Afterword	96
Acknowledgements	97-98
Meet the Author	99
Meet the Artist	100
Meet the Publisher	101

Foreword

This is an airing of dirty laundry. Mine and theirs. I think it's important to note that I'm not angry anymore. I think it's important to note, I'm not sure I ever was. If I've learned one thing, it's that we are made of only stories. I hold mine in my palms and spine and throat. Take them between your teeth gently; remember we are all such fragile things. If I've learned two things, it's that sometimes the life raft and the sinking ship are a direct reflection of each other. Similarly, there is love and pain threaded through every page, pulled tightly, just like grandma taught. I hope you find the stitches that feel the most like home and add them to your armory. A preemptive thank you, for trusting these words with your time. A preemptive thank you, for helping me keep them safe. To the ones who pulled me down off the tops of parking garages, you are the only things that make these pages turn, and to the ones who know the tops of parking garages like I do, I hope this can be your parachute.

Allow Me to Introduce Myself

I am 5 feet 6 inches
Which is 4 inches taller
Than the other women in my family
But 5 inches too short to be taken seriously

I weigh too much or too little
Depending on how many shots of whiskey
Sit in my father's throat
I like to wear t-shirts 3 sizes too big

I have brown hair
But it used to be blonde
And it used to be longer
And I used to wear dresses
And I used to like that

I have brown eyes
But in the sun, they are gold
And they have wrinkled corners
Hidden behind blue-light glasses

I am one part boxes I don't fit in anymore
One part skin covered in scars and ink
One part I am no longer sorry for that
And one part say my name with respect

My childhood home
Was a graveyard of contradictions

I am not good at things like

Playing doormat
Or sitting with my legs crossed
Or knowing when I should leave

I am not the first addict
But I am the first college graduate
Not the first grandchild to snip green beans
But the first one to wave goodbye to the garden

I am a brave thing

Some call me a flight risk
Some call me chest caved in
But no one
Has ever called me easy to forget

Unapologetically Woman

I don't hate being a woman but
Sometimes my skin stretches in ways
I did not give it permission to
And my eyes read more invitation than warning
And the curve of my spine
Resembles my mother's too closely

Sometimes my hips feel like
Unwanted house guests
Inside of men's cargo pants
And my hands keep a running tally
Of all the times they've been considered too small
My heart will cave the first time the right person
Calls me pretty
I store teardrops safely in their tear ducts
Because boys don't cry but neither do tough girls
And I've pretended to be both

I skip like a broken record
Every time I say that soft and weak
Are not synonymous

I don't hate being a woman but
It took 7 years to learn the title can stand on its own
Without needing the prefix— victim
Or the suffix— survivor

I am human just as much as I am woman
I am holy just as much as I am whole

Nightly Routine

I splash cold water
On a face I don't recognize anymore
Repeat "I can do hard things" in the mirror
Like a prayer

I wonder if there's a god who answers those
And if the person staring back at me
Believes in them

But Don't Call Me Weak

Call me poet with a bone to pick
Call me silencer on a loaded gun
Call me cemetery full of empty graves
Call me forest fire fully extinguished
Just smoking
Call me open book without an ending
Call me fist fight without the knockout
Call me angry
Actually call me hurting
Actually call me healing
Call me lover
Call me safe
Call me everything you're afraid of

Take Me out of My Skin

I have been carving your name out of my skin
With broken tequila bottles
For the better part of 7 years
Attempted to make space
Between my thighs for gentle hands
And space behind my ribcage for gentle hearts
I have failed at both
More times than the words "don't cry"
Dance through the shadows of my thoughts
In your voice
I have talked about it a lot in therapy
Used anger as a morning affirmation
As an addiction
As a religion
And my therapist says that the most important tools
Serve many purposes
That it's okay to use and reuse them
As many times as I need

I hold this toolbelt in my throat

But sometimes it's in the space
Between dusk and dawn
And sometimes it lives in the corner of half-smiles
And sometimes it sits with me in the shower
When I can't seem to peel myself off the floor of it

It's been 7 years since I've gone into the bar
On the corner of St. Joe Center and Clinton
6 and a half since your last attempt

To clean up the mess you made
4 since I left the city you threw a black veil over
And named it death

I am not angry anymore

Sometimes I wake up at 3 am
And feel my bones lying right next to yours
But I've gotten better at holding myself
Sometimes I see you
In every white middle-aged man's face
At the grocery store
But I've gotten better at focusing on my reflection
On the doors of the frozen aisle instead
Sometimes it hurts too much to think about
Other times it pours out over coffee with a stranger
And my therapist says
That there is no right way to heal

But that I am doing just that

Pretty in Pink

I walk alone at night
Pretending like I am the most powerful thing
On these streets

We love rose-colored glasses

Thinking: I wish a man would try
But rewind two hours
And you'd see me frozen to the sidewalk
Wondering if I would become a statistic—
Again

But they paint the world so pretty

Like my knees looked pretty
The first time they kissed pavement
And I'm wondering if this was all just a love affair
Gone wrong

But you're different now

I say with conviction
She didn't know what she was capable of then
Didn't know that she had teeth
Or at least how to use them

But you really do believe people are good

And believing they are good is why
I still sleep with a nightlight

And why there are people I still can't look in the eye
And why sometimes I can't tell the difference
Between the barrel of a shotgun
And the stem of a dandelion

You shouldn't walk alone at night

And I guess you're right

How to Write Poetry:

- Peel back the layers of your skin like an onion, slowly. Ignore the way your eyes swell and sting and seep
- Take a hacksaw to your sternum. Crack it open and split your ribcage in two. Step back and watch your heart erupt in an array of bloody colors.
- Unravel your intestines. See how far they stretch and if they ever cross a finish line. If they don't, see if you can stretch them a little bit farther.
- Suck the air out of your lungs like a helium balloon and watch them shrink and shrivel. Throw them into the air and hope they still know how to fly. Let them fall to the ground.
- Study your hands. See how they feel around your own neck. Squeeze until you're white-knuckled.
- Take your skeleton out of the closet. Sit it in front of the mirror and force it to stare into its own reflection. Force it to break its jaw into a smile. Force its reflection to smile back.
- Reteach your legs how to run. And then run. Remind them that they can go as far as they'd like. Remind them that it's okay to turn back and come home.

Whiskey or Lighter Fluid

I scan the liquor cabinet
Searching for the thing
That tastes the most like home
Not to drink of course
Just to clean out old wounds

Did you know that if a tree (glass)
Falls (shatters)
In a forest (kitchen)
While both kids are upstairs sleeping
Everyone hears it?
Have you heard that version of the story before?

Take my hand
Let me show you
What it feels like to crack wide open
What it means to run back
Begging to be fed from the same hands
That removed your seat from the table

My therapist asks why I stay and I say
Because it doesn't matter who dropped the match
And who dumped the kerosine
If the whole thing
Was always going to go up in flames anyway

2,000 Days in Recovery

I feel myself start to slip-
But don't you remember how pretty things look
Through the bottom of a bottle?
Don't you remember
When you were the loudest one in the room?
Things are quieter here
Sounds muffled by the ashes of a past life
I promise I'm still trying to put her to rest

I'd like to think I can see myself
Staying a little longer here
Planting a garden
Driving for miles
Sitting on porch swings
I'd like to think it'd be easy
That all my cards would fall into place
Open hand laid out on the table
Royal flush

And I guess there are worse ways to survive
Meaning
I've tried to survive in all of the worst ways
So this time
I dig my heels into the sand
Knees bent
And wait for the next wave to crash
Did you know that the sky still spins
Like a kaleidoscope
When your vision is clouded by saltwater?
This time

I put that to my lips instead

How to Survive a Gunshot Wound (When You're the One that Pulls the Trigger)

Let the shrapnel puncture your lungs–
You've been holding your breath for so long
Choking on the exits and the exhales
This time let the air escape

Let it graze your heart
Separating the part that hates yourself
More than it loves her and try again
Don't tell her a part of you went missing
Just say you finally feel whole

Let the shattered pieces float up to your throat
Let them pick the lock on your voice-box
Let them make all the noise you never could
You weren't built to be a quiet thing

Let the shards rest inside your skull
Clear out the clutter
And make a bed for your new house guests
Sometimes the thing that's supposed to kill you
Saves you without you knowing

Lie down
Apply pressure on the entrance wound
Wait for the ones who will crowd in claiming hero
And when they ask to see
Where the bullet came out
Ask them
If they've ever felt what it means to be alive

To the Trees Outside the Window, I could See if it wasn't so Dark

I want to write about the pine trees
About how–
Even covered in snow
They never complain about the added weight

It reminds me of my bones
Bending
Snapping
Breaking
But who would hear it if they did?

The First One on Grief

Grief knocks at a door
I haven't opened yet
Skips the pleasantries
Sits down at the table and
Immediately demands to be fed

So I gather up the scraps and
Place them in front of its mouth
Grief says it's still hungry
So I make a grilled cheese
Just like grandma taught me how and
Grief reassures I'm getting closer to its craving

So I toss a salad of
Folded laundry and
30-minute phone calls with 3,000 miles in between
Mid-day naps on the davenport and
Lemonade in the front yard
The quilt we sewed together and
Lessons in German
Chinese checkers and
Boxes full of old photos
Not enough hugs and
Too little time and
I serve it

Grief asks where I'm hiding the rest
So I carve out one third of my heart and
Place it in its lap
Snap my spine in half and

Place it at its feet
Pull out the pit in my stomach and
Spoon feed it
Cut out one of my Achilles and
Dangle it in front of grief until it salivates

I say take it all
Take it all
Take it all

We All Get Out Alive and Other Lies I Tell Myself

Coffee tastes better black and at room temperature. Home can be anywhere that has a night light. I haven't thought about hurting myself at all. Not once. Growing up is exactly the way they said it would be. I'm just learning at a slower pace. My childhood bedroom door doesn't need to be locked anymore. Nothing bad will ever happen here. Nothing bad ever has. I don't care about the amount of likes I get on my Instagram posts. I don't miss her. Especially not when it snows. Especially not when I hear *the phone number you are trying to call is no longer in service*. I'm not afraid of collapsing in on myself. Or bleeding out. Or finding out I was never really here in the first place. I will eat three meals a day. Starting tomorrow. I'll also start wearing a seatbelt. Even in the uber. This is the end of a stanza not the end of a story. I don't miss her. especially not when I'm stumbling over the last lines. It is enough to wake up and still have a heartbeat. It is enough to wake up and still have a heartbeat.

Track Star

If you ask my mother how I became a runner
She'll say it's the only thing
That didn't come straight from her—
That this lead-footed
Pedal to the medal
Fingers tapping on the steering wheel girl
Could not have gone further
In the opposite direction
She was a gymnast
Used to shape-shifting her body for perfect tens
That she was raised to be
Flexible and
Poised and
Quiet

She'll say she doesn't know
Where I got these pigeon toes
Or this long stride
But if the cemetery out back could talk
It's voice would stretch for miles
I was fast and
Strategic and
Quiet

There are other parts of us that intertwine
Like our eyes
Glossy and unfocused after 3 beers
Our laugh
When the joke's at our own expense
And our love for the song Amazing Grace

She'll say that she raised me
But the only pieces of her I have left
Are the ones that still need glued back together

The first time I stepped onto a track
I felt another part of her get lost in the wind
And the first time I laced-up my spikes
I thought
Maybe not all sharp objects
Are meant to be used as weapons
Maybe the one holding the gun
Is more to blame than the bullet
Maybe I dodged this one

We speak in hushed tones
Carefully side-stepping around
The callouses on our feet
And the hot coals underneath them
But then the announcer says
"Runners to your mark"
And only one of us stays behind to get burned

I Call it Going Back, She Calls it Coming Home

I wonder what it'll be like now

One year and six versions of myself later
I'll go back
I'll watch the quilted fields from 30,000 feet
As they drape around the place
That failed to keep me warm
And wonder
If there just wasn't enough room underneath it
For a thing like me

I'll turn back into the child
She was always so afraid of
And she'll turn back into the broom and dustpan
He'll have 4 whiskey-cokes before he can say hello
In a language I'll understand
And we'll fall back
Into the same cookie-cutter conversation:

High school sports
     (Instead of how my heart feels)
The weather
     (Or if I ever found what I was looking for)

I'll train this Venus Flytrap mouth to smile more
Convinced that razor sharp teeth look less deadly
When framed in something softer
I'll sit at the end of the dock
The water will look like glass

And I'll wonder which of the two of us would shatter
If I jumped
I'll bow my head for a goodnight kiss
She'll mistake it for a prayer
And I'll mistake it for an apology

And neither one of us will correct the other

Among the Unlikeable Parts

They say it takes 66 days for a behavior
To become automatic
But I would argue that science
Is no match for determination

I mastered the art
Of making this body a graveyard
In seconds

Does anyone know how long it takes
To break a habit?
Or at least how to break a tombstone?

Photo Album Confessions

I hold that picture like my hands
Are the only things that can keep it
From ripping right down the middle
Trying to find where she still fits inside this body
Or if she ever grew into that cowboy hat

A hard line drawn between What Is and What Was
Studying the lines in the wrinkles of his forehead
And wondering if those two things
Have always been the same

Change happens
In the moments you least expect it

When the tips of fingers meet the bottoms of bottles
And the whole ship sinks

When the girl meets her match
And they realize they have the same reflection

When the story take a turn no one saw coming
And the whole house crumbles

I Love You but…

Our house has never been big enough
To keep me safe
And to keep you warm at the same time

I don't have any bones left for you to pick
If you stay, won't you be bored?

You fall asleep with your shoes on
And your car key safely fastened to your belt loop

You've taken up too many of my therapy sessions

I can't end up like my mother–
Reciting apologies like a prayer

No one wrote a survival guide for this
And I forgot to leave breadcrumbs
To find my way home

I can't remember what my own skin feels like–
This reflection is a stranger

This story was never one
You were interested in finishing

I let you turn this body into a demolition site
And I need to start rebuilding

There isn't enough room for the two of us
To keep our heads above my flooded lungs

I want to relearn how to float

I want to reteach my hands
How to hold things gently

I want to rewrite a version of myself
That doesn't flinch
When I finally allow my head
To be filled with all light

If the Timing were Right the Story Would be Boring

Just this once tell me what I want to hear
I want to crack your spine
And search through all the footnotes with my name
Go back to that one time
I said that one thing
And you asked what the hell I was thinking
But why waste time with eloquence
When there's satellites on the tips of our tongues

What if just this once you call my bluff and I fold
I want to breathe you in
And choke on all the words you won't say
Like that one time
We set that one rule
And we both said thank god
Because our fingers were getting slippery
Trying to hold on

You say a "what if" is loudest
When whispered
But you never said what happens
When it's screamed

Don't Talk to Me About the Weather

Instead / talk to me about the sidewalk / cracks / how to float around them / how you float around me / talk to me about the endless possibilities of every / yes / every / fuck / every / my god / talk to me / about your favorite last / line / how your tongue got stuck / just before / you turned the page / bookmark that / we'll come back to it / talk to me about the shadows / how you learned to dance / how you curl up with a glass of wine / or tea / talk to me / talk to me about how / when the first light / peaks / in through the cracks / and it's so goddamn / beautiful you can't help but to talk about the weather / talk to me about where I can find / the whole of / you / when the sun goes back down

Holier than Thou

I have spent more time planning my eulogy
Than my wedding vows

Which is to say
I've always thought of myself
More as a thing to be remembered
Than a thing that can be loved

This body

Has skinned its knees on more bedroom floors
Than Hail Mary's

Which is to say
I've never thought of myself as a good girl
But more of a broken record
Skipping on all the rough edges

They say

Treat your body like a temple
But what if it was built on top of a burial ground?

On Tattoos and Apologies

They ask why I would damage
A perfectly clean body

I say because I like being broken

I will never apologize for the times
I have been more art than girl
More canvas than bomb shelter
More museum than coffin
But they see this ink as a reflection
Of their failed American dream
White picket fence wrapped in barbed wire
I wonder how many times
They trip over it themselves

They ask why I would do this to myself

I say because maybe
I never got tired of sharp objects
Or maybe because it hasn't felt like mine
Since I was 4
Or maybe because it's easier to decorate
Than a tombstone

I say they're just tattoos

Butch Church Girl

I don't know much about god
At least not anymore
But I know how many miles there are
Between here and my heart (2,063)
And I know how much closer to heaven I feel
When I land there

I don't know much about hymns
At least not the ones in the backs of pews
But I know how many days it's been
Since my lungs learned they could sing (147)
And how loud they've been every day since

I don't know much about praying
But I know
There are better things to do on your knees
I don't know much about worship
But every time I put my hands up
She's there to hold them
I don't know much about god
But I do know
What it's like to believe in something infinite

Playing Dress Up

I'm looking for a boy
Bleach blonde curls and a smile
Just soft enough to smooth out the edges
He was a small thing then
Covered in butterfly hairclips and river water
Always wondering
Why I taught him to sleep with the lights on

Have you seen him?

I can't remember exactly when I lost him
But I know it was somewhere
Between sister and stranger
If you see him
Can you tell him I'm looking?

Tell him to follow the Oreo breadcrumbs
To the basement stairs
I'll be sitting in the sound of car doors slamming
At 3:05 A.M.

Tell him I'm sorry
For stealing his quarters
And for the amount of times I haven't called
Tell him I'm waiting
Somewhere between sinner and sister
And I just want to talk

Tell him I'm not much different
All string-bean arms

And stories tucked underneath my tongue
That I'm the small thing now
But that I never dropped the weight

If he ever asks: have you seen her?
Can you tell him I'm here?

Black Sheep

She asks for a yellow sundress
So I give her a yellow button down
And hope it reflects the sun in the same way

Church girl turned sinner
She asks if god still lives in my body
I ask her the same

Disappointment threaded into every check up
I sew my lips up tight
Just like grandma taught me how

Keeps my room dressed up the same way I did
She asks when I'm coming home
I tell her I've been home ever since I left

The Body Keeps Score

My body and I have stepped into the ring
More times than I can count
And I have a history of being a sore loser
The starting bell rings once
Loud
And my fists shape-shift into something
I've been taught to be proud of
I make a list of every escape:
A forfeit
Three rounds
Or a knockout
And for the first time I'm wishing myself more time
So I stand there
Fists raised in a half-hearted attempt
To make them useful
But the final bell rings once
Twice
Three times
And it's over

I couldn't even destroy myself properly

Learned Behavior

Every time
The pastor looks me in the eyes
While he tells us to repent our sins
And the English teacher at the end of the hall
Doesn't say hello

Every time
Dad calls her a friend
Waiting for my loud mouth to correct him
And the volleyball coach
Determines my playing time
Based on who I kiss in the off season

Every time
The regular at the bar says
I just haven't met the right guy yet
And his friend says
I won't know until I try

Every time
The server loses our order
After seeing who's hand I hold across the table
And mom sends a card with the 23rd Psalm
Reminiscing on the good ol' days

Every time
I interview for a new job
And they tell me to cross my legs like a lady

Every time

I come back
And my baggy cargo pants are gawked at
Like a circus act

Every time
I look in the mirror
And try to erase the versions of myself
They created for me

I wonder
If they worship their god with the same mouth
If they hold their offerings with the same hands

Under a Microscope

She said she likes feeling small
So I wrap myself around her
Chest to chest and

Tell her about the universe
How we could fly through it infinitely
Without coming into contact
With a single other thing
How even then
I would diverge from the course
If it meant her and I would collide

Tell her about the sequoias
How their skin is fireproof
So when they burn
They burn from the inside out
How even then
I would let her turn me to ash
If it meant I could keep her warm

Tell her about a lifetime
How the world never stops turning
Despite the amount of times
We've tried to put our laughter in a freeze frame
How even then
I will find her in the next one
So I can wrap myself around her one more time

Things to do Between the Hours of 12 and 1 AM

Tell yourself you'll start a new poem / call yourself failure when you don't / unclench your jaw / over and over and over / read the first 5 pages of 3 different books and try to find anything that means something / get lost in a Tik Tok hole about glitches in the matrix / notice how tight your boxers feel around your waist / replay the conversation with your mother / worry you didn't ask her enough questions about herself / be mad at yourself for not raising your brother to be better / finish your notes for therapy complete with problem and solution / masturbate / google: how close can you get to the sun without bursting into flames / 1.3 million miles / for 30 seconds / imagine the upstairs neighbors' dog is roller skating over a bed of marbles / make a goal for tomorrow: be better at telling people you love them / talk yourself out of buying a scale on amazon / thank little you for always walking around barefoot / check and recheck your alarm / 6:01 AM / wonder who you'll be 5 hours and 51 minutes from now

Almost Untouchable

I say here are my hands
I can make them fit into yours
If I break a couple fingers
I'll trade shoes with you
Even if yours are too small
Or too worn
As long as your feet don't blister
Mine are too calloused to know the difference
My father gave me strong shoulders
You can have those too if yours get tired
I promise mine are not filled with anger like his are
Here is the key to my house
And the oldest scar on my wrist
And all the reasons I can't sleep
Here is the first time I saw my reflection
And hated it
Here is the last time I tried to leave this world
In the same fashion I entered it—
Bloody and screaming
Here is my side of the bed
I've kept it warm
Here are my outstretched arms
I have been told they are a soft place to land
Here is my chest
You can sink your teeth in
But only if they are around my left ventricle
Here are all the times you've put periods
Where there should have been commas
Don't worry
I edited it for you

Fantasizing About the Men in the Room

The man sitting next to me
Is drinking a Jack Daniels—neat
The man behind the mic
With the rainbow guitar shoulder strap
Is singing a song about love and the moon
And I'm not sure which one I'm more drunk off of

When I was a kid
I would stop breathing in my sleep
My parents would stumble up the stairs
And connect my lungs to a machine
I guess I've always known what it means to survive
On oxygen that isn't mine

The man with the rainbow guitar shoulder strap
Can beatbox
And play the flute
And make cricket noises using just his mouth

The man sitting next to me
Is on his 3rd Jack Daniels neat
And I wonder what the sweetest thing
My lips have ever tasted is

When I was 12
I snapped my right wrist snowboarding
4 days later I had perfected a mid-range jump shot
With my left hand
Which is to say
I know what it means to love a thing enough

To want to reteach your body how to love it
Even when you're broken

I wonder if the man sitting next to me
Has someone waiting for him at home
I wonder if she had to remind him
To take off his shoes
Or if she pulls him in for a kiss
When she smells the whiskey

When I was 22 I decided to run away
High on the idea of being a thing nobody knows
What I mean is
I'm really good at making a home
Out of places I've never been

It makes me wonder if the rainbow shoulder strap
Ever knew it would make music
Or if it took one look at the guitar and thought:
Damn just another thing to carry

Before You Say Yes

I've learned to present this body
As an apology letter:

*i'm sorry, yes, there are still places
inside these bones even i won't visit
i'm sorry, no, don't put your hands there*

*i'm sorry, yes, i still sleep with the lights on
i'm sorry, no, there is not an inch of smooth skin left
for your tongue to trace*

*i'm sorry, yes, i think i'll always be searching for the
next place that feels like home
i'm sorry, no, i'll never be able to have a glass of
wine with you*

*i'm sorry, yes, there are still some pieces i am
trying to glue back together
i'm sorry, no, i will never be a thing that is
completely habitable*

Evidence that You're Alive

The staggered breath before the sob / extending your toes in the damp morning grass / and curling them in pleasure / the moment someone truly sees you for the first time / words scribbled on pages of warped leather bound notebooks / the smell of freshly brewed coffee / the roughness of your hands running along the walls of the 100-year-old brick house that sits on the corner / the softness of the nape of their neck / the childhood picture of you your grandmother still has hung by a magnet on her fridge / the ignorant belief that things won't always be this hard / grief / love stories— the real kind / the weight of your resentments / the floating that comes after the forgiveness / the muddy paw print on your rug that just won't wash out / asking for help / curiosity / about the world and about yourself / the terror right before the fall / the sacredness of the hands that catch you

The Talk of the Century

Grandma taught me that most things
Can be mended with needle and thread
Which is probably why
I feel so tethered to her spine
She's 98 now
And I know that I can't make time move backwards
But I'm hoping it slows down a little
Like her steps have
She says she's proud of me
And I tell her that I can't get my grilled cheeses
To taste like hers
No matter how much butter I use
She says she misses me
And I tell her that I have more wrinkles now too
Because I got so used to her holding me
I haven't taught myself how to do it yet
She says she loves me
And I tell her that she has 100 more years
Left in her

I'm learning how to use a needle and thread now
I'm learning not to flinch
When I stick my finger instead
Because she never did
I'm learning that these hands are strong
Because she's the one that sewed them together

Shit No One Actually Cares About

I let hair grow in places where we're taught it shouldn't and last night I cried during yoga. Tonight I thought to myself, you know what I haven't done in a while? Caught a lightning bug. I wanted to tell someone about this. I love sending cards and I think that that is the most adult thing about me. I walked past a man grabbing the shoulders of his friends asking them "how does your soul feel?" I told someone about this. I think I'm always going to be an addict. I lost my favorite t-shirt months ago only to find it curled up on my best friend's pillow. She offered it back to me, but I like the thought of being in two places at once. I left the crew neck too. Make that three. I always know where my heart is by the way it writes poetry. I've been told that there is an age you reach where you're too old to die young. I like the way my therapist responds "say more" when she knows I'm tip-toeing on the surface. You can tell a lot about a person by the way they catch or kill a spider. I have this one friend that I tell all my intrusive thoughts to and one time I saw 22 airplanes during a baseball game. Sometimes I catch myself wondering how many times you've fallen asleep with the lights on. I started running because she walked a mile a day from ages 95-99 and I guess I'm thankful that my legs can still tell my feet to move. One in front of the other.

First Date Confessions

She said:
You have a way of turning pain into poetry
She said:
It's not pretty
It's not neat and clean like your organized stanzas
Syllables falling in line
One after another after another
A perfect distraction

She said:
You aren't healed like your poetry makes you seem

Playing Hide and Seek with Yourself

Do not ask yourself if I am still made of anger
Or where I've hid it in my body
I've dug my way through cemeteries
Looking for that answer
And always come up with empty graves

Steps to Making a House a Home:

- Hide the empty whiskey glasses behind the smiles in the family portrait that hang above the mantle
- Stop setting out 4 plates at dinnertime
- Start only pouring 3 glasses of milk
- Memorize which one of the stairs creaks (3rd) and how much time you have to rub the sleep from your eyes and prepare your shaking fists (20 seconds)
- Pick out a plot of land in the cemetery out back
- Spray paint your name in the grass, right there
- Stick a post-it note on the wall in every place he calls you "bitch"
- Make a maze out of these hallways so there are plenty of places to hide
- Or vantage points to attack from
- When it finally starts to feel more air than cage, move
- Repeat

Steps to Making a House a Home: Part 2

- Leave your demons at the front door no matter how many times they knock no matter how many times they try to break in
- Build a bed out of the people who have told you they loved you and meant it
- Buy all your favorite snacks
- Eat them on your kitchen floor at midnight because this kitchen is not a graveyard
- Recycle your tears and use them to water your plants
- Keep a tally of all the times you've heard "I am proud of you" in permanent marker on your mirror
- Recite "I am proud of you" out loud in your mirror
- Put the dog bed right next to yours so you always wake up knowing what it feels like to be unconditionally loved
- Lock your car at night— you won't need a quick escape
- Stay there

Urn

Grind my bones to ash
Tell me again that I look pretty on your mantle
And when they ask what's inside
Tell them you haven't figured it out yet

The plaque that sits below me should read
House of god
Locked diary
And injured racehorse
In no particular order

Allow the dust to collect and cake and settle
Claim I am too heavy to be moved
And when the whole house burns
Tell them you did everything you could

Finding a Means to an End

She connects the dots between every piece of skin
I've ever tried to cut out like a constellation
Calls it home
Says it's whole despite the holes
Says if I ever need to find myself
I won't have to look far
That she's dog-eared every page
I've been too scared to read
And put the book in her lap
In case I ever need a safe place to rest my head

I spent the first year with my face in the concrete
While learning how to skateboard
Which is to say
I've never been afraid of falling
But I keep waiting to stand up
And find skinned knees
She says
Welcome to the school of unlearning

I'm learning that the apple falls far from the tree
What I mean is
I'm learning how to be loved gently
What I mean is
Her skin is soft like silk sheets
What I mean is
She loves me like the moon
Says she wants a one-way ticket to the side
No one else has ever seen
And I'll let her

There was a time when I fantasized about jumping
From my favorite parking garage
Which is to say
I always knew my story would end
Without a parachute
But her hands were a landing I never saw coming
She says
Welcome home

I'm learning home
Is made of more heartbeats per second than walls
What I mean is
It's cliche to say home has never been a place
What I mean is
She loves me despite the chipped paint
What I mean is
She loves me

And I
Have never been a love poet
But I love her
So I take her hand and say
Let me show you what it feels like to touch the sun
And she lets me

First Date and a U-Haul

I can make a bed out of the smallest spaces

Which is probably why I didn't hesitate
To set moving boxes down
On the floor of your lungs
To start unpacking books
On the shelves of your ribcage
To hang string lights around your heart
And sit cross-legged at the base of your sternum
Palms outstretched
Soaking in the warmth of your words
Before they turn to ash

When We Ask Why

I've spent a lot of time asking god
Why they gave me this body
Only to spend so many years
Wanting a way out of it

Can't you see this body is strong?
They said

This mouth
Has sang battle cries and bedtime prayers
Been the loudest thing in rooms
Built with soundproof walls
Been the softest touch in places
You can't talk about without blushing

These hands
Have held your mother's tears and your own neck
Been award-winning carvers
With no trophy to show for it
Been the things that hold hers
When she's too tired to hold herself

These knees
Have carried the weight of your family name
And every step you've taken
In the opposite direction
Been the things that catch your head
The moment before it hits the ground
Been the pilot that has taught you flying

This body
Has seen the inside of churches and caskets
Been the contractor and the demolition team
Been your own worst enemy
And all of the reasons you've survived

Surviving on Scraps

I've made a habit of starving myself

I've never asked for a seat at the table
I'm not greedy
Instead I'll play dog at your feet
Not expecting—
But hoping that you'll be a little careless

You'd be amazed at how little I need
To make a meal

Construction Site

I could say
It's hard to build a home with rotted wood
But instead I say
I've been collecting the framework for a decade
I'm just not finished yet

Mouth or Muzzle

How much do you think your own voice is worth?

Is it enough to bring someone to their knees
Then back to their feet in a standing ovation?

Have you ever yelled "echo" in a concrete tunnel
and counted how many times the word comes back?
How it gets softer and softer until it disappears—
Tell me, which pitch sounds the most like coming home?

If you could bring water to a boil using just the
words you wish you would have said
How many seconds do you think it'd take to feel the burn?
How long would you leave your hand in the pot for
the sake of feeling anything but nothing?

If I had to guess, I would say the gunshot is always
louder than whatever the bullet lands in,
But I've always been too afraid to pull the trigger.

If you had to guess, would you say your voice is
worth more as a silencer?
Or the thing that makes them scream?

I teach kids to yell into their pillows when they can't
control the fire in their lungs.

I realize now, I should never encourage them to snuff out a flame,

Especially their own.

An Astronaut's Love Letter

I have written more eulogies
Than love letters
Made a graveyard out of my bones
More times than I've sewn my skin back together
Because sometimes saying goodbye
Is easier than saying I'm sorry

I have spent more mornings
Scrubbing nightmares off my skin
Than reading the newspaper
Made crossword puzzles
Out of my resentments
And called myself a master

I have lived far past my expiration date

And I often find myself
Daydreaming about the stars
How they burn
And explode
And fall
How even in death
They are something to be in awe of

And we are so unaware
Of the power we hold
Our ability to bend
Just shy of breaking
Bravery laced with raw determination

So I sew my skin back together
Again
Not for myself
But for the stars
To show them that even in life
We are something to be in awe of

Loving in My Mother's Language

My mother taught me how to love like quicksand
Like stick your toes in
Watch it crawl up to your lips
Like swallowed whole

Which is to say

I will stay
With one bullet loaded in the chamber and say:
Make sure you have the safety on
You know there is a one in six chance
This could all blow up
And you've never been a fan of messes
I will stay
With the gun pointed at my head and say:
Put that down and let's talk
You know your words
Are the most lethal weapon anyway
I will stay
Face down on the same living room floor
I've picked your breaking bones up off of and say:
Give me five minutes to sew this skin back together
and throw a rug over the stain

My mother taught me how to love like regardless
Like above all else
Like hand over flame
                Keep it there
                              Say thank you as it
                    Burns down to bone

Weathering the Storm

Dating someone with depression
Is like playing a game of Russian Roulette
But when it comes to her
I will always make sure
The gun remains unloaded

Life is Silly

Because humans are made of 60% water
But 3,500 people drown every year

Because someone once said it doesn't get better
And that's the best part

Because you can't remember any of your past lives
But places you've never been feel familiar

Because I haven't used algebra once
Since I got an A in 8th grade

Because we got jealous of the birds
And built our own version of wings

Because lightning doesn't come from the sky
It comes from fingertips

Because there's always grass that's greener
But some grass is also dead

Because there are people that feel warm
Like a shot of whiskey

Because there are people who feel like hot tea
And sometimes those two people are the same

Because you can't put a Band-Aid on broken ribs
But they can still be put back together

Because there are 7.9 billion people in the world
And not a single one of them has all the answers

Because we never will have all the answers

Because trying to find them is half the fun anyway

10 Places You Can Find Me

1. Cross-legged on the floor of a used bookstore
2. Wrapped around their finger— whoever they may be
3. Underneath a waterfall pretending I've never been afraid to get my toes wet
4. On the front lines of a war between head and heart with no armor
5. Buried in the covers convincing loneliness this bed isn't built for two
6. In front of a mirror searching for the flattest angles
7. In the space between paper and pen
8. With my therapist— gluing pieces back together
9. At the top of any and all parking garages
10. Lost in the mountains trying to find my way home with only half the amount of breadcrumbs I remember leaving behind

If I Should Ever Go Missing

Look for pieces of me in everything I've ever loved
Used bookstores and
Puppy breath and
Her
Carve my name into every park bench and
Porch swing and
Freshly poured sidewalk
Follow where the bird's song is the loudest
Retrace my footprints
To the first place I called home and
The last place I cried
You can find me in the yellow

If I should ever go missing
And you find yourself missing me
Read back the poetry I scribbled
Onto my headboard
And know that I will always be with you
While you sleep

A Love Letter to My Hips

How brave you must be
To jut out in all the wrong places
At all the wrong times
Unapologetic and loud
Begging someone to see you

How proud you must be
For defying all the ways
In which you've been told to keep quiet
Screaming at the tops of men's cargo pants
And the bottoms of a size-too-small t-shirt

How lonely you must be
Waiting for someone to look at you with affection
Or really anything but an apology
I'm sorry

Today I will tell you that I love you
Tomorrow I will try to believe it

Happy Poem

I walk in and it smells like coffee
The bed is unmade as it usually is
Because life is messy sometimes
The dog's curled up in the chair
I'll complain about the black hair
On the beige blanket
And how the pillow
Will never regain its original shape
But I'll smile at her anyway
The sound of cars driving by is almost amusing
A reminder that there is life outside of me
And I'll sigh
Have you ever missed something
While standing in the middle of it?
I take a picture
Attempt to freeze time
Or at least slow it down a little
I'm a beginner at being happy
But I turn the record player on
Dance around the kitchen
Ignoring all the dirty dishes
And remember

I'm a fast learner

Between Slab City and Salvation

I wonder how many people have walked away
thinking that I am the most broken place they've
ever been—

If they took one look at my crooked rib cage
Barely guarding my blue-tarp'd heart
And saw that what appeared to be a welcome sign
Was actually a warning
That there is no electricity to keep us warm here
And the lack of a front door
Makes it easy to leave without making a sound
If they saw that the road between
My splintered floorboard feet
And shoes to protect theirs
Stretched for miles
Or that I'd crafted a bed out of scrap metal
And things I wish I would have said
Would they think to themselves:
How could anyone make a home here?

I wonder how many people have walked away
thinking that I am a masterpiece—

If they took one look at the shattered windows
And knew I just wanted to let the light in
And saw what appeared to be just shards of glass
Were actually the wind chimes
That sang them to sleep
If they held onto these rusted radiator hands
And found that they still gave off enough heat

To keep theirs warm too
Or that the kitchen table was held up
By all of the times I begged for an exit route
But forced these legs
To go a few more miles instead
Would they think to themselves:
Would she let me make a home here too?

Kintsugi

My hands have never known
How to hold things gently
But she makes me want to learn—
Makes me want to reteach these bones
That they were built for more than breaking

She covers the cracks of my fingers with hers
A place I never knew I could make a home in

Maybe
She will teach me how to love these cracks
While she fills them with gold

First Step

Today I decided to count the books on my shelf
Instead of the scars on my wrists
Flip through every dog-eared page like a prayer
Remembering that each cracked spine
Was an act of survival

There is more than one way to stay alive
Run my fingers through the thin layer of dust
Trying not to think about my bones
Becoming just that

Today I decided to mop my floor
Erase every muddy footprint
In an attempt to put What's Left of the past
Just below the surface

These days I am doing more than just surviving
Slide across the kitchen in my socks
Remembering all the times my feet were more
Quicksand than ice skates
Thanking them for not being that

At least for today

Other Firsts

I retrace my steps back home
Attempting to get back a broken routine
I surrender

All half-cocked smile with palms in the air
Miracles, I'm learning
Are not all that rare if you have your eyes closed

And is it really such a bad thing?
To have an X on a map
You love more than your own skin
Who said soulmates have to have a heartbeat

There are things I wish I could go back
And do again for the first time
But I'm learning that second and third times
Keep the wheels turning in the right direction

What god calls lessons and they call mistakes
I call war
Because a white flag never pumps enough blood
To both head and heart at the same time
This is where beautiful things go to be reminded
That they are more than just beautiful things

Where every stone left unturned
Is actually a stone dropped into a wishing well
So I hold my breath and dive back in
There is still so much more time

Cheers to the End of the Patriarchy

Although we are made of gold
We are not trophies
You can sit on a shelf in your study
To dust off when you feel lonely

We are no longer the generation of trophy wives
But the generation of breadwinners

Soul City

I tell them
I think I'll live here one day.

They say
*slow down little wandering thing, you're getting
swept away by the current without testing how deep
the water is.*
I tell them
*driftwood bones don't get to decide when they land
but they always seem to land at the exact moment
you need a bridge.*

They say
but what about the gray?
I tell them
*what about the green? and plus there are plenty of
good things that are gray like the moon and flat
round stones that are perfect for skipping and the
line between unhappy or just bored.*

They say
but won't you be cold?
I tell them
*I have mastered the art of rubbing two ice blocks
together and creating fire.*
I ask them
why do you think my hands are always so warm?

They say
but I'd miss her, that little wandering thing.

I tell them

there hasn't been a single day that I don't miss her too, so when I find her— and I know I will, I'll send her back for coffee every once in a while.

I Have to Tell You..

Sometimes I want to exit this world
Quicker than you could reach for my fingertips
And beg me to sit back down
But sometimes I want to wake up before the sun
And watch it kiss the horizon good morning
And sometimes I want to shove my nose
Into a pile of old books
And breathe them in like I'm drowning
Sometimes I want to walk barefoot in the gravel
Because it's impossible not to feel completely alive
With a reminder in every step
Sometimes I want to lay in bed all day
Listening to the sound of the cars driving by
And make up stories about the people in them
Sometimes I want to hold her so tightly
That we start to share a heartbeat
Sometimes I want to laugh
In a quiet room
At the wrong time
Because I thought about how ridiculous it is
That earth is the size of a grain of salt
When compared to the galaxy

I guess what I mean is
Sometimes I want to stay

Correction: Not a Fever Dream

Home doesn't scare me like it used to
Driving past old smoke spots
Remembering tree stumps like scaffolding
From homes we built when ours got too loud
We were cool back then
Or we at least thought we were
With our 99 cent slushies and 99 cent vodka
Rushing to third period
Like we had nowhere else in the world to be
The river
The barn
The cemetery out back
Held more secrets from the living
Than it ever did from the dead
My family name
Was either a curse or a legend
Depending on who was telling the story
I dig up old roots just to confirm my suspicions
I really did grow here
This wasn't all just in my head
Sometimes places feel like fever dreams
When you leave them
But I'm older now
And the pain in my side only aches
When I haven't been to therapy in a while
And the string between here and there is frayed
But not completely broken
So I drive slow
Savoring the smell of fresh cut grass
And open space

I call it home with only a minor hesitation

A Love Letter to Myself

If I had to write a love letter to myself
I would probably say something
About how I'm a little kinder now
Than I was four years ago
But still not as kind as I could be
That it's brave to keep trying
And bravery is a form of love
If you're looking into its reflection

I would say
I don't know how to write love poems
I know even less about what it means
To love a thing properly
What I mean is
I have always been a hands-on learner
And maybe the hands that taught me
Weren't always kind
But I know a lot more about unlearning now

I would say: drive safe
And: make sure you eat today
And: stop being so careless with your heart
Because there has never been
Only one way to love
I've just always chosen ones that hurt or leave
So I've practiced the same on this body
More times than I'd like to admit

If I had to write a love letter to myself
I'd say that my summertime freckles

Are what's led to my obsession with space
I would say that my voice
Is what led me to cities
I now want to make a home in
I would say that the stretch marks on my hips
Are here to remind me
Of all of the versions of myself I've outgrown
I would say that my heart
Has simultaneously loved too much
And not enough
But it still beats

I would say
I don't know myself enough to love every part yet
But that the mirror lies a lot less
I would say I'm proud to still be able to love at all

I Am Poet

As in
Breaker of my own bones for sport
As in
Truth teller wrapped in a blanket of metaphors
As in
Healing.. but with a masochistic twist
As in
Time traveler
As in
Loudmouth
As in
My own worst enemy
As in
Romanticizer of the unimpressive
As in
Martyr in the war between head and heart
As in
Sleepless.. but always wide awake
As in
Arsonist with no exit plan
As in
Carver of my own skin
As in
Keeper of no one's secrets
As in
Biblical.. if the bible was written by a feminist
As in
The one your mother warned you about
As in
Competitor in a losing game

As in
Architect of more nightmares than daydreams
As in
Founder of ghost towns
As in
Copilot with an engine on fire
As in
Carpenter.. with a saw for a tongue
I am poet
As in
Lover
As in
Protector
As in
Still alive

I Never Asked to be a Survivor

In fact, if I had a choice, I would be a writer. Pinprick every fingertip just to say: I create art from blood and flesh and bones. Metaphors spilling from my pores and analogies dancing off my tongue. I would write something that means something. As if anything means anything. I would cradle trauma between college-ruled lines. Shove a pencil through my bun to look cool. Walk with my nose in the air and when someone stops to ask: What books are you reading these days? Reply: Nothing. I am too busy working on the next New York Times best seller. Complain of writer's block. Complain of deadlines. I would write stories of girls that had too much to drink and too little self-preservation. I would make it sound so pretty. Collect pen caps to measure progress. Throw crumpled paper balls into a trash can. Still count the pages that make it in as wins. I wouldn't be afraid of some tall man in some dark alley because he would be too afraid of becoming my next antagonist. If I was a writer, I would change the title from: "Survivor" to "Just a Girl." Call it a fairytale.

Supernova

The visible stars in our milky way galaxy
Actually went dark around 10,000 years ago
But because Earth sits 10,000 light years away
It makes the perfect light show for a night cap

This is the best way to describe my PTSD
The best way to describe how
I went from this living breathing thing
To collapsing in seconds
How I went from the life of the party
To no longer being able to support my own weight
But I wish it were that simple
See

My rapist knew my middle name
And my favorite drink
And the breed of my childhood dog
Which is to say
Our atoms were crushed so closely together
My core disintegrated under the pressure
I tried to counteract the sudden imbalance
With other chemicals
But that only put the downfall in slow motion
Like the dream where you're falling
And falling
And falling
And you can't wake up
But you're tired

I couldn't feel my legs

But I could feel the carpet burns underneath them
Couldn't see his hands
But they still burned every inch of skin they touched
I couldn't remember our last conversation
But I knew for a fact it ended in no

A star explodes approximately every 10 seconds
Which is almost the same thing as saying
A woman gets raped every 2 minutes
But just like the stars
After the first few
We just stop talking about it
Move on to the next completely outrageous thing
Like trans athletes
Or the red-neck's rights to own assault rifles
But I will not stop talking about it
I will scream
And collapse
And explode
For as long as it takes to get someone to hear me
Because if I am not allowed to forget
Then I will not allow you to forget either

So when you see me now
Know that I am not just a cluster of rocks
Floating in someone else's orbit
Know that I have traveled thousands of lightyears
Dodging planets and half-ass'd apologies
But that I made it
Know that the person who had this body first
Died almost a decade ago
But that there is light

Dripping through all the cracks
Know that I am more stardust
Than I ever was survivor
That a supernova ain't got shit on
What I'll do next

So take this as a warning
Because when some stars explode
They turn black hole
And swallow everything in their path

Afterword

Sit. Breathe. Listen. Put hands to chest, or hands to feet, or hands to head. Remember you are still here. Remember there is still so much time.

Acknowledgements:

Cover Art: Kyra Rolleri

Thank you for not only your art but your friendship, your nomad lifestyle that constantly inspires me to leave regular life behind, and for being Myka's best auntie. I will always be more than happy to share a mailing address with you, because it means you'll always be close to me.

Photography: Sara Dobbins

Thank you for taking me under your wing during week 1 of living in Seattle, and for not letting me sink. I am forever grateful for your friendship, your optimism, and your monthly astrology lessons.

Supporting Organizations:

Poets Underground:

Thank you for being the first company to put my name in print. I will never forget that feature performance where you held my hand on stage and called me family.

San Diego Poetry Slam:

Thank you for guiding me through the last 5 years of (attempting to) perfect my craft.

HipHopandPoetry:

Nothing builds a creative family quite like traveling the country together. Thank you, Mike Xavier, for giving us all that opportunity.

Supporting Characters:

Maura Barrett

      Thank you for always knowing I can do and be more. I love you.

Nicole Antonacci

      Thank you for letting me sprawl my pages (and myself) out on your living room floor, and for providing the chocolate while we work.

Misty Schoof

      Thank you for reading and rereading every poem I've ever sent you. Grateful to call you friend AND family.

Logan Kroezen

      Thank you for keeping me alive for the better part of a decade.

Influential Poets Turned More:

Rudy Fransisco

Monarch The Poet

Mercedes Wallace

Tiff Hubbard

Meet the Author:

Brooke (she/they) is a queer spoken word and slam poet originally from Fort Wayne, Indiana. Their poetry career started in 2019 at the San Diego Poetry Slam, and they have since then had the opportunity to perform and compete in various cities across the country such as: Baltimore, Las Vegas, Seattle, Chicago and Los Angeles. They have also had the privilege of being able to merge their passion for advocacy and the arts by being a guest speaker at human rights rallies and abortion rights fundraisers, as well as at local high schools. This is their first full-length published manuscript, but you can find pieces of them in the following anthologies: Poets Underground Vol. I, Not Ghosts but Spirits Vol. II, and the San Diego Poetry Annual 2022-2023. When Brooke is not writing or performing, you can find them somewhere in the mountains with their puppy and a dead car battery, just hoping everything works itself out.

Meet the Artist:

Kyra Rolleri aka Kai is a nomadic artist originally from Germany. Kai has been living fully nomadic for 3 years. Constantly on the move, they find inspiration from their travels across diverse landscapes and cultures. With a passion for blending artistic traditions with contemporary design, Kai creates unique tattoo designs that reflect their global experience. Her artistry not only captures the essence of her wanderlust but also resonates with clients seeking personal and meaningful pieces of art. You can find more of their work on their Instagram page: @inkventure_tattoos

Meet The Publisher:

Poets Underground is a Movement
Sunny & Anthony Azzarito, the Founder/CEO and COO of Poets Underground Press LLC. Their passions drive from their love for God, their 5 children, their inclusive community and the arts. The couple runs writing events, open mics, writing & preforming workshops, retreats, partners with schools and community service events; in great effort to foster healthy individuals and communities. Known for their partnership publishing programs, they welcome all aspiring writers to apply.

poetsundergroundpress.com

www.ingramcontent.com/pod-product-compliance
Lightning Source LLC
Chambersburg PA
CBHW050915160426
43194CB00011B/2423